Leadership Expertise
Mastering Influence.

Prriya Kaur

Copyright © 2020 Prriya Success Academy

All rights reserved.

ISBN: **979-8-61-728757-0**

"Leadership is the single most important ability anyone can master. Anyone and everyone can become a leader. Whether you realize it or not, there is a power waiting to be released inside of you. It is the reason you won't settle. The reason you strive to better yourself, and to better those around you."

- Prriya Kaur

CONTENTS

	Acknowledgments	I
1	Introduction	Pg. 1
2	Human Needs Psychology	Pg. 3
3	Transformation Skills	Pg. 19
4	Principle 1 – Understand and respect their world.	Pg. 23
5	Principle 2 – Connect personal power and get leverage	Pg. 31
6	Principle 3 – Changing Limiting Patterns	Pg. 39
7	Principle 4 – Identify and define the problem	Pg. 45
8	Principle 5 – Make the change and find empowering alternative resources	Pg. 51
9	Principle 6 – Condition the change until it becomes a habit	Pg. 57
10	Principle 7 - Associate with higher purpose and connect to an Empowering Environment	Pg. 63
11	Measuring yourself as a Leader	Pg. 69

Disclaimer:

Before you invest here in the form of time, efforts or money, be sure to carefully consider the investment objectives, expenses involved, possible risks and probability of changes. All investment involved may be at risk including loss of principal investment. Past performance does not guarantee future success and results. The parties contributing to this product are not registered/licensed investment advisors. Their opinions and comments are their own. There are not meant to be taken as investment recommendations and advice. Additionally, their opinions and comments do not reflect the opinions of, nor should they be attributed to, the copyright holder.

The plans drew are simply the results of huge research done in this field and are not just our personal recommendations. We only deliver our teachings around the world which are helpful to people which is clear from the results of our research. We advise you to use highest and due diligence before you invest money in any course.

All rights reserved.

Without limiting the rights under copyrights reserved above, no part of this publication may be reproduced, introduced into a retrieval system, or transmitted, stored in any form, or by any means (electronic, recording, photocopying, mechanical and otherwise), without the prior written permission of the copyright owner of the manual.

Dear Achievers:

Welcome to the **Leadership Expertise** and congratulations on being one of the extraordinary souls to commit to mastery. Mastery is a state when we constantly produce results beyond and out of ordinary. It is a journey to take you along a path that is both arduous and exhilarating, it is to bring unexpected rewards, and newfound truth, and learning about yourself and others. Becoming a master not only allows you to grow personally, but it enables you to contribute and excel beyond your own expectations.

This course is strategic in teaching you **excellent leadership skills** and more in-depth understanding of the **Psychology of Human Need** along with transformation tools for creating lasting change. Before you are able to effectively create change in others, you must understand the psychology of why we do and what we do. Then you are able to use the appropriate skills and tools designed to create lasting change in your life and that of others too.

With the help of this module, you will discover the resources and tools that will help you **create conscious growth** and **take your career to the next level**. You will learn unique skills in this program. It helps you both personally and professionally, as you will have the ability to influence the thoughts, feelings, actions, behaviours and emotions of others.

Neuro Linguistic Programming (NLP)

NLP is a science developed by Richard and Dr. John Grinder in their effort to model the communication strategies of effective therapists and business people. For past three decades, Tony Robbins has discovered the patterns that shape all people - regardless of status, background and nationality. His work is the mastery of a school of psychology that created **Human Need Psychology**.

By applying the NLP principles and Human Need Psychology, I have created **7 principles**, which help you understanding the patterns behind all human behaviour with which you can help people change their thoughts, feelings, actions, behaviours and essentially the results that make up their life. In addition, when you have the ability to influence others, you have the capacity to be a true leader for a positive change.

I am both **inspired and privileged** to share my expertise of **Leadership Expertise** with you. I am blessed to be a part of your life. We embark on this program together, let's mark commitment to both give and succeed at the highest level. Let's continue the journey and, as always, remember to live with passion and never, never, never give up until you achieve the results you want.

"Giving up is an easy option; standing up for yourself and fighting to achieve your goals is not everyone's cup of tea. Be the leader of your own thoughts and win over every situation."
- Prriya Kaur

INTRODUCTION

"Good leaders are made, not born. If you have the desire and willpower, you can become an effective leader. Good leaders develop through a never-ending process of self-study, education, training and experience." - Jago, 1982

"A process whereby an individual influence a group of individuals to achieve a common goal." - Northouse, 2007, p3.

1.1 What is Leadership

The ultimate goal of leadership, is about **progress**. It is the ability to make things happen, maximize resources and inspire. It is the capacity to create an environment where people thrive and results are achieved. It is an extraordinary quality that solves problems and gets the things done.

Leadership is the ability to influence the thoughts, feelings, behaviours and actions of those you lead.

Leadership is the tool to help people deal with specific issues and accomplish their goals. In essence, make new decisions and take new actions.

This is a journey that leads us to develop the distinctions of **effective leadership** and helps us to **understand** what makes us do the things we do. It is a path of creating lasting change and making the decisions that can change your life and the lives of others.

HUMAN NEEDS PSYCHOLOGY

"We are leaders who engage the Force for good; who are unreasonable in our expectations and demands of ourselves; and who are constantly training ourselves to be in that magical state where this force is flowing through us. And, as a result, we awaken all those around us."
— ANTHONY ROBBINS

If you really want to create **a lasting change** in your life and other people's lives and take your business to next level, you need to **find out** why do you do what you do.

Moreover, if you are going to influence somebody else, you have to understand what influences them first. Once you begin to explore another person's model of the world, you can start to investigate the makeup and patterns behind their actions and how you can influence them for a positive change.

If you are going to influence someone, you have to know what already influences them.

2.1 You must understand HUMAN NEEDS PSYCHOLOGY.

Human Needs Psychology provides an answer to the age-old questions- why do human beings do things they do? How is it that one human being sacrifices his own life for another person? While another person murders a stranger for sheer pleasure? What creates a Charles Manson or Nelson Mandela, A Jeffrey Dahmer or John F. Kennedy, A Unabomber or Martin Luther King? What is the force that drives and shapes all our emotions, actions, qualities of life and ultimately, our destinies?

No matter who you are in the world, or what you do, there is a **common force** that is driving and shaping all your emotions and actions. It determines the quality of your life and ultimately, your destiny.

There are **6 fundamental needs** that every person has in common, and all behaviour is simply an attempt to meet those 6 needs. The drive to fulfil our 6 human needs is encoded in our nervous system.

Every person finds a way to meet these 6 needs by hook or by crook. Any activity, action, or emotion that fulfils at least 3 needs at a high level becomes, in effect, an addiction. Likewise, people have positive, negative and natural addictions. There is always a way to fulfil a need, the skill lies in finding a sustainable way to fulfil it (and in a way that gives you more pleasure than pain).

2.2 THE SIX HUMAN NEEDS

The four primal needs:

1) Certainty - The need to know that you can avoid pain and gain pleasure.

Everybody wants stability about their basic necessities which leads to certainty of availability of the basic requirements, such as

- Food
- Housing
- Comfort
- Control
- Consistency
- Learned helplessness
- Identity
- Completion
- Faith/belief in guidance

2) Uncertainty/variety - The need for the unknown, for change, for new things.

People feel a need to change their state to exercise their body and emotions. Therefore, they seek variety through a number of means: Stimuli

- Change of scene
- Physical activity
- Alcohol
- Drugs
- Sabotage/pick a fight
- New relationship
- New job
- New location
- Stimulating conversation taking on new challenges
- Learning
- Rethinking of focus/tempo of focus

3) Significance - Feeling unique, important, special or needed.

Everybody needs to feel special and important in some way. People will seek significance through obtaining recognition from others or from themselves. When people feel insignificant, they may make themselves feel significant by getting angry or doing some of the following actions:

- Tear others down
- Violence
- Negative identity, disease/disorder
- Showing off material possessions
- Showing off accomplishment (high education)
- Showing off new knowledge and skills
- Showing unnecessary care or extraordinary companionship
- Scarcity (as criteria for creating a feeling of uniqueness or important)

4) Love/connection - A strong feeling of closeness or union with someone or something.

Humans need to **feel connected** with someone or something – a person, an idol, a value, a habit or perhaps a sense of identity. This connection may take the form of love, or just of intense engagement. For instance, one can feel connected by means of an aggressive interaction or:

- Sympathy via sickness/injury
- Negative behaviour (crime, drugs, smoking, etc.)
- Get others to comply with your requests for relationships (family, friends, intimacy, sexuality, etc.)
- Spirituality
- Be in natural surroundings (in nature)
- Join a team/club
- Self-sacrifice
- Beauty/art
- Pets

The two Spiritual needs (primary, essential, ultimate):

5) Growth - An expansion of capacity, capability, or understanding.

Everything in the universe is either growing or dying, there is no third alternative. People are spiritually satisfied, unless their capacities are expanding.

If you help others to be fulfilled, you will be fulfilled.

Consistently give to others that which you wish to receive.

You have within yourself the resources to feel complete, fulfilled in all six categories, in any situation, regardless of how others respond to you.

6) Contribution - A sense of service and focus on helping, giving, and supporting others.

Just as people cannot survive without others contributing in some way to their happiness (no baby grew up on its own), they cannot be spiritually fulfilled unless they are contributing to others as well.

What differs among each of us is how we value these needs. Typically, a person has two needs that they value the most. The way you can determine your top two driving needs is by evaluating which needs tend to show up when you are under stress, fear, anxiety or difficulty. Regardless of what you think, you want or what you would like to value, operationally, when in the midst of challenges, what tends to show up?

2.3 Exercise

1) Out of the 6 human needs (certainty, uncertainty/variety, significance, love/connection, growth, contribution), what are the top two that are driving you? Remember, this is not what you value the most; it is which two you live most operationally.

_____
_____
_____
_____
_____

2) Think of an area of your life that you're really pleased with. Why are you pleased with that area? Capture it. You will notice, that area likely matches your core expectation of how life should be at least at a basic level.

_____
_____
_____
_____
_____

3. Think of an area of your life that you are not pleased with. Why are you not pleased with that area? Notice how your life conditions in that area do not match your personal blueprint. What can you do to shift it?

_____
_____
_____
_____
_____
_____

2.4 Exercise:

Discovering your six human needs:

All human beings are consistently seeking to meet the 6 Human needs, but we all tend to value two more than the rest. For example, someone who values certainty will live a radically different life than someone who values uncertainty/variety. Similarly, someone who focuses on significance will interact with others very differently than someone who's number one need is for connection/love. When you know which needs you value the most, you can better understand the choices you make, as well as your emotional patterns.

1) What are the ways you get certainty? Uncertainty?

Certainty		Uncertainty	
Positive	Negative	Positive	Negative

2) What are the ways you get significance? Love/Connection.

Significance		Love/Connection	
Positive	Negative	Positive	Negative

2.5 Exercise:

Discovering your Six Human Needs

1) Of the six Human needs, which two have you been valuing most?

_____
_____
_____
_____
_____

2) What are the consequences of valuing those needs in that order?

_____
_____
_____
_____
_____

3) What do your top two needs need to be now for your life to transform?

_____
_____
_____
_____
_____
_____
_____

4) If you made that change, what would transform in your life?

_____
_____
_____
_____
_____
_____
_____

2.6 Human Emotions and Behaviour Psychology

Have you ever wondered what controls and determines the quality of our lives?

Answer is - emotions, physiology, focus, language, meaning.

What controls our lives are the meanings we associate with the things in our lives, which are shaped by our own personal psychology and our world view (the beliefs and values that we have created).

Once meaning is established, each individual will have a pattern of emotions that they associate to this meaning as their natural way of coping.

All meanings are driven by our individual patterns of emotions. We all have patterns of emotions.

THE TRIAD		
(the three forces that shape all human emotions and behaviour)		
The source of all emotion is a constellation of three forces		
Force 1	**Force 2**	**Force 3**
A pattern of	A pattern of	A pattern of
How you use your body (Physiology) ➢ Breathing ➢ Hydration ➢ Volume (Tempo of voice)	**Whatever you focus on, you will feel.** ➢ Question (Primary question) ➢ Values	**Language** ➢ Meaning ➢ Language ➢ Beliefs ➢ References ➢ As soon as we put words to an experience, it changes the meaning we experience.

2.7 THE TRIAD AN EXAMPLE FINANCES

My Goals	The Behaviour
What driving need are you trying to meet with this behaviour? I try to give myself comfort and pleasure: I like to reward myself by taking myself out of pain and into pleasure. **What are the results and consequences of your current behaviour?** I hardly save any money: most of the time, I do not have enough money for what I need.	**What is the behaviour you are committed to change?** I like to change my behaviour to stop spending much more than i earn. I do not save and do not invest. **The Emotions** **What do you really feel?** I feel frustrated, panicked and then overwhelmed and depressed. **My behaviour Triggers** Shopping with friends, they are spending too much money and working too many hours and weekend parties. **The Emotional Triggers** Feeling deprived, always depriving myself of things. Feeling panicked about my lack of time and lack of resources. Feeling exhausted and overwhelmed from working too much and not having any leisure time. **Drivers (Reference, Submodalities)** **Reference** (my dad and my friends do it all the time) **Submodalities** (picture is dark, I see picture in black and white. Pictures are around me)

THE TRAID: THE SOURCE		
1. A pattern of Physiology How are you currently using your physiology?	2. A Pattern of Focus and Belief What do you focus on?	3. A pattern of Language What phrases, words questions and metaphors do you use?
• I cry • My facial muscles are tight • My tone of voice is not very warm and friendly • I kind of hold my breath and breath shallowly.	• I do not have any money left in my pay check to give up for investments. • I will never be able to pay off all my debt. • Everyone is using a credit card, so it is okay for me to do. I have to figure out my long-term career goals before I can make any real money. I can fall back on credit cards if I have to.	I will never get over my head, so it is okay to build up some debt. I am so broke. I am so poor. There is nothing I can do. I have to get a grip. How am I going to pay for this? It is not good as compared to my friends.

MY OLD DISEMPOWERED SOLUTION	MY NEW EMPOWERED SOLUTION
1. What driving needs are you trying to meet with this behaviour? I try to give myself comfort and pleasure: I like to reward myself by taking myself out of pain and into pleasure. **2. What are the results and consequences of your current behaviour?** I hardly save any money: mostly, I do not have enough money for what I need. **The Behaviour** **What is the behaviour you are committed to change?** I like to change my behaviour to stop spending much more than I earn. I do not save nor invest. **The Emotions** **What do you really feel?** I feel frustrated, panicked and then overwhelmed and depressed.	**1. What driving needs are you trying to meet with this behaviour?** I want to have sense of certainty that I have comfort in the financial area of my life. I am charged and making intelligent choices as a sense of growth. **2. What results do I really need?** I want to have a clear spending plan that allows me to be certain that I am not financially stressed and save 20% of what I earn. **What is the behaviour I am committed to?** I want to have 20% automatically deducted from my payback, so I never see it or spend it. I join some investment club and have fun investing. **The Emotions** I feel happy, in control and intelligent about my choices, feel proud and independent.

My behaviour Triggers

Shopping with friends, they are spending too much money and working too many hours and weekend parties.

The Emotions Triggers

Feeling deprived, always depriving myself of things. feeling panicked about my lack of time and lack of resources. Feeling exhausted and overwhelmed from working too much and not having any leisure time and it is a quick pick me- up.

Drivers (Reference, Submodlities)

Reference (my dad and my friends do all the time)

Submodalities (picture is dark, I see picture in black and white. Pictures are around me)

THE TRAID: THE SOURCE

1. A pattern of Physiology		2. A Pattern of Focus and beliefs		3. A pattern of Language	
Old	New	Old	New	Old	New
How are you currently using your physiology? I cry My facial muscles are tight My tone of voice is not very warm and friendly I kind of hold my breath and breathe shallowly.	What new Physiology will empower you? My body is filled with energy and excitement. My eyes light up and i smile My physiology is certain. I am relaxed I breath more deeply and slow	What do you have to focus on and believe in? I do not have any money left in my pay-check to give up for investments. I will never be able to pay off all my debt. Everyone uses credit card, so it is okay with me to do. I have to figure out my long- term career goals before I can make any real money. I can fall back on credit cards if I have to.	What do you need to focus on and believe in? There are so many ways to make money. I can manage my expenses. I am totally capable of taking care of myself and achieving my goals. I am disciplined, I need to raise my standards for what I save and invest. I surround myself with who are happily investing. I can learn, be in control and have fun.	What phrases, words, questions or metaphors do you use? I will never get in over my head, so it is okay to build up some debt. I am so broke. I am so poor There is nothing I can do. I have got to get a grip How am I going to pay for this? It is nothing as compared to my friends.	What new phrases, words, questions or metaphors will empower you? Right, this is easy Investment is fun like shopping. Who can I learn from? What another way can I make money? I am proud of myself for taking control. I can do this and i want to do this.

Each of us, individually, has a unique personal **psychology** and **philosophy** of life, what we call our model of the world. So, if we trade the three, the tipping point of meaning affects our state and the decisions we make in the moment, then make our model of the world. The three forces of Destiny affect our decisions in the long term. Our model of the world is the filter through which we experience life. These three forces create our view of the world; the way we interpret life and the decisions we make.

It shows that emotional pain is always the result of constructing and creating a disempowering meaning within yourself. By changing our physiology, focus, language and meaning, we can shift to a more empowering state and make more empowering decision.

THE TRIAD EXERCISE FOR YOU

Your Current Pattern	Your New Empower Pattern
1) What is the driving need you are trying to meet with this behaviour? What are the results and consequences of your current behaviour?	1) What are the driving desires and needs you want to meet now? What results you really want?
2) The Behaviour. What is the behaviour you are committed to changing?	2) The Behaviour. How do you want to behave in this situation in order to achieve the desired results?
3) The emotions. What are you really feeling?	3) The emotions What are you committed to feel?

Notes:

TRANSFORMATION SKILLS

"Real transformation requires real honesty. If you want to move forward – get real with yourself."
- BRYANT MCGILL

The **purpose of 7 principles** is to give you the power to influence yourself, and others, and to consistently produce your desired results by understanding how a person makes decisions. Moreover, mastery of the 7 principles gives you a specific sequence, core and tools to follow or to help someone permanently transform so that they reach the deepest level of fulfilment possible as well as the greatest opportunity to grow and contribute to others.

It helps you make great decisions and gives you the ability to instantly and consistently take action, even in stressful, harsh or unfair conditions. Besides it, mastery of these steps requires understanding to effectively use the motivational force behind all human behaviour – the need to avoid pain and the desire to gain pleasure.

The 7 principles based on **Neuro-Linguistic Programming (NLP) and Anthony Robbins** act as tools to understand how specific causes are set in motion by our beliefs, values, rules, thoughts and actions, and theme effects that determine the directions and the ultimate destiny of our lives.

3.1 Neuro-Linguistic Programming (NLP)

In 1970s, Richard Bandler and Dr. John Grinder did some pioneering work on the science of mind called NLP or Neuro Linguistic Programming. They worked on communication strategies and consulted some highly successful therapists and businessmen to arrive at astounding results. They opined that the internal representations in the human mind had a big role to play in the experience and behavior of human beings. They inferred that what we human beings experience is not the reality but 'only a representation' of the actual reality. As per NLP, "The map is not the territory." Simply put, it means that the map is only a representation of the actual territory.

Literally, the term NLP or Neuro-Linguistic Programming can be understood by looking at the following break-up of the term:

Neuro – Neuro refers to our nervous system where we receive, process and interpret the information received by our mind from the external world through our five senses of vision, hear, touch, smell and taste.

Linguistic – Linguistic refers to the language or communication of neural representations, their coding, interpretation and order of occurrence in our mind.

Programming – Programming refers to our ability to organize the non-verbal communication, signals and neurons to achieve the results that we desire. For doing this successfully and also to our full advantage, we need to understand the following basics –
(a) The working of a particular segment of our mind.
(b) The language that our subconscious mind understands.
(c) The ways to reprogram our subconscious mind.

3.2 The 7 Principles creating Lasting Change

(Transform life where it counts the most)

Principle 1: Connect, understand their reality and respect their world (you have to understand who you are dealing with and what exactly is shaping them).

Principle 2: Connect personal power and get leverage (find out what makes change happen).

Principle 3: Change Limiting Patterns and get the edge (changing focus, meaning, language, perception and physiology).

Principle 4: Identify your controlling force (in solvable terms).

Principle 5: Make the change and find empowering alternative resources (access empowering ways to meet your six human needs and the emotions you need to strengthen).

Principle 6: Conditioning the change until it becomes a ritual (condition new decisions, thoughts, emotions and new actions).

Principle 7: Understand the purpose of life and connect to an empowering environment (make sure the environment supports it).

Notes:

PRINCIPLE 1
Understand and respect their world.

"Make improvements, not excuses. Seek respect, not attention."
- ROY T. BENNETT

Hersey and Blanchard (1988); the act of guiding and influencing people to achieve desired outcomes.

Besides, when you want to have an impact as a leader on any human being, then the first thing you need to know is what already influences the person you are trying to influence.

You must know and understand:

Their **6 needs** especially the top 2 needs.
Their **model of the world** as what drives them and,
Their **beliefs** about what has to happen to make that work.

4.1 Introduction:

There are seven categories of beliefs that affect how people create meaning in their life. Remember, even if you value the same needs as another person, what is totally unique to you is how you decide if these needs are met and ultimately, the quality of your life that guides you to understand your and their model of the world and how to respect their world.

4.2 Categories:

1) Global Beliefs

These are very important aspects of our lives, because they control many decisions in our life. **Understanding global beliefs** helps us understand what generalizations people create which control the many decisions they make in their life.

Example:

What is the reward in life?
What creates pain?
What is the purpose of life and death?
What are the resources available to you?

Time
How much is a short/ long time? Is time scarce or abundant?
Where do you spend your time (past, future, present)?
Money, people, love, emotions, life metaphors.

Your Guiding Force:

What is your favourite phrase in life?

    Life is about ...... life is not about ....

    Life is always .... life is never ....

    The purpose of life is ......

2) Identity:

It is simply the way you describe yourself to yourself, the belief you use to define your own individuality. Identity is the combination of the beliefs about what you are capable of, who you are, and how you distinguish yourself from everyone else in the world. There is no other force this powerful in human personality.

Example:

Who are you not? Who are you?
What is your life about? What is your life story?
How are you like/not like them? Who is your role model?
How can you expand your identity now?

Your Guiding Force:

Identity

You are ...you are not...

You are made for....

You believe....

Your most important beliefs are......

3) Values/Deepest Desires/Greatest Fears:

These are the states that move away from (in order to avoid pain) or towards (in order to gain pleasure) to give them context.

Example:

What is important to you about a name as the context?

What is important that you would do anything to avoid ?

Your Guiding Force

You want ......

You desire....

You need....

You must have been....

You do not want....

4) Rules: the source of Heaven/ Hell Within:
These are the determining factors in our decision about which behaviour to utilize in order to experience our values. Some rules have a higher priority because violating them causes greater pain.

Examples:

Threshold: must/must not/must never/must always

Personal standards: should/should not/should never/should always

Possibility/impossibility: can/cannot/can never

Rules of intention: will/will not/will never/will always

Global beliefs: is/is not

Your Guiding Force:

You must not ....

You must never ...

You must always ....

Others must not ...

Others can not ...

Others must never ....

What has to happen in order for your values to be met?

5) Vehicles and Virtual Villains:

These are the methods people use in order to meet their needs; the way they get from where they are to the needs they want. They can be positive, negatitive, or natural.

Examples:

What are the ways you try to meet your needs? (e.g. money, career, physical body, relationships, religion, problems, suffering, pain, helplesses, food, drugs and so on)?

Does this vehicle have a positive, negative, or netural consequence?

Your Guiding Force:

What are the ways you meet your needs?

1) For certainty?
2) For significance?
3) For variety/uncertainty?
4) For love/connection?
5) For growth?
6) For contribution?

6) Situation Specific Beliefs:

These are situation-specific beliefs such as the organizing beliefs behind the way a person evaluates a specific situation or context.

Examples:

An infield fly rule (a specific situation where it is okay to violate your rules). As people can believe that cheating on their spouse is wrong, but there may be a context (e.g. if their spouse cheated on them) where they believe it is ok. Or is there a context in which your beliefs are different (e.g. a lie vs a white lie)?

Is there a specific situation where you would do something against your values (e.g. physical assault vs self-defence)?

Your Guiding Force:
1) You violate your own value when you ....
2) You break the rules when ....
3) You break your own rules ....
4) Do you have a filter for your actions?

7) Metaprograms:

They help us understand how a person processes information. Metaprograms are another filter through which we process our world. Knowing people's metaprograms can help you offer the type of information that will help them make an effective decision.

There are a variety of ways we process information. For example, one type of metaprogram is whether you have an internal or external frame of reference. One way to elicit this is to ask, how do you know when you are really good at something?

Internal people look to themselves to make decisions, external people talk to others. To motivate internal people, find out what is important to them; to motivate external people, use testimonials and statistics to show what others think.

Your Guiding Force:
1) What are the emotions you experience most often? How many emotions do you experience at least once a week?
2) What are the feelings that you have?
3) What are the challenging emotions you feel once a week?
4) What are the empowering emotions you feel once a week?
5) What makes you fearful? Scared?
6) What makes you sad?
7) What makes you angry?

Notes:

PRINCIPLE 2

Connect personal power and get leverage (find out what makes change must happen)

"You gain strength, courage, and confidence by every experience in which you really stop to look fear in the face. You are able to say to yourself, 'I lived through this horror. I can take the next thing that comes along.' "
- ELEANOR ROOSEVELT

5.1 Introduction:

According to Porter (2012), **leverage** is often the single **most important element** in creating a **long-term change**. There are many therapies that can work to change. But sometimes, therapeutic approach will not be effective unless you have enough reasons to change.

We have noticed that we often fail to change until we reach threshold because we associate a lot of pain to our old behaviour that continuing it is unbearable. At this point, we must associate pleasure to make the required change in order to access powerful leverage immediately and use our personal power.

Below are some powerful key distinctions for getting leverage:

Connect and leverage - What makes change a must target of focus:

- There are only six sources of motivation: The Six Human Needs.
- Ask questions that create pain and pleasure
- Framing
- Global solutions (changing belief which stop them to take actions)

5.2 Framing - The basic model for change:

In order to create lasting change in somebody, you can change:

1) How they feel (their emotions)

2) What they are doing (their behaviour)

TO CHANGE BEHAVIOUR, IT ALL GOES BACK TO THE TRIAD

The Tipping Points:

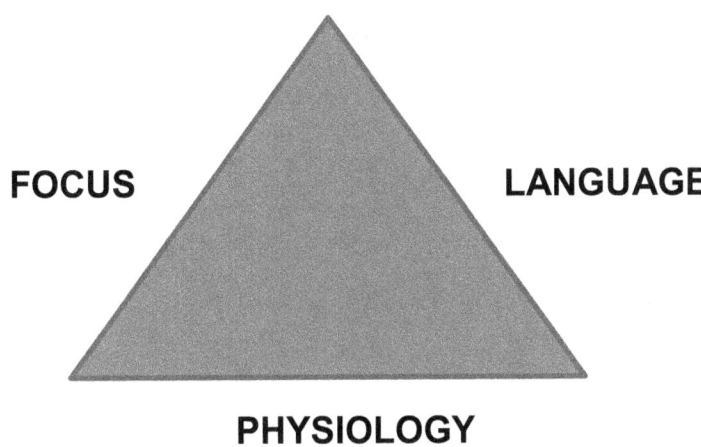

Using framing to obtain leverage:

To change emotions, you must first change the meaning for people. There are **three practical approaches** you can utilize when influencing meaning which are **Focus, Language and Physiology.**

5.3 Pre-Framing:

When you tell someone in advance what to pay attention to and what it is going to mean to them. This is one of the most powerful tools of influence.

Two keys to pre-framing:

1) Frame things in a way that relates to their benefit.
2) Ask questions to which you already know their response so that you can control the frame.

Example:

You are trying to get leverage on your team at work to align with the new company mission.

You could say, "I need to talk to you about a huge change in the company that will affect you all. But my hope is you will like the direction we are heading in".

Or you could say, "I am so excited to share the direction and next level our company is heading in – we now have the opportunity to have more impact along with more opportunities and resources to reach our customers".

Exercise:

What statement do you think would get more leverage in getting people to align with your new company mission?

In getting leverage, you can use pre-framing to set up in advance what you want someone to focus on.

5.4 Re-Framing:

When somebody already has a problem and you change what it means by having them see it through another frame of reference.

There are 2 type of re-framing:

1) **Context Re-Framing** – to change what something means by having them see it in another context, in another situation. Show them how something that seems to be a problem is one situation is a benefit in another.

Example: My 16 years old daughter is stubborn and will not do what others tell her to do.

Re-frame: She certainly will not fall into peer pressure and will stay true to who she really is.

2) **Content Re-Framing** – to change the imagery surrounding an image in the past by scrabling it so that they do not see it anymore, or to give someone new information that they did not have so that their new understanding transforms the previous meaning.

Example: "I owe the IRS $1 million this year".

Re-frame: "Wow! you must have really made a lot to own that much".

3 keys to an effective re-frame;

1) Interrupt the pattern

2) Use questions

3) Align with their beliefs.

When asking people questions, come from a state of curiosity, not judgment. No one who feels judged is going to change.

5.5 De-framing:

When somebody is caught up in a particular element and you simultaneously destroy their frame of reference.

For example, if you were trying to sell a house, but someone objected that the house was too expensive, you could de-frame this response by saying, "I am also concerned whether you can qualify for the loan".

5.6 Four keys to framing:

1) Rapport: before you try framing someone, you must have rapport.

2) Questions: Do it in the form of questions whenever possible.

3) Interrupt their pattern: Have a frame that interrupts their pattern. When you tell a story, people go into a trance, or when you ask a bizarre question that has nothing to do with what they are doing, it will crack them up and put them in a new state.

4) Constantly change their physiology without their awareness.

5.7 Global Solutions (changing belief which stops them from taking actions):

When people are failing to change, it is most likely that they have some sort of belief system that their action, behaviour, or pain is on a level meeting their needs. In other words, the reason they do not change is because they think changing their state from pain to pleasure would take away something that is meeting one of their needs. If you are looking for leverage to get people to make a shift away from pain and into pleasure, then you need to help them find something that they value more than the pain. Show them now their current behaviour is causing pain, and find a global solution to create a new behaviour or action that will empower them by meeting their needs and giving them pleasure.

How to be responsible (empowers you to take the responsibility of change):

Taking responsibility is one of the best measures of a person's power and maturity. It is also an example of beliefs supporting other beliefs, of the synergistic capabilities of the coherent system of beliefs. If you do not believe in failure, if you know you will achieve your outcome, you have nothing to lose and everything to gain by taking responsibility. If you are in control, you will succeed.

Because another attribute great leaders and achievers have in common is that they operate from the belief that they create their world. The phrase you will hear time and again is, "I am responsible" or "I will take care of it". It is not coincidental you hear the same viewpoint over and over. Achievers tend to believe that no matter what happens whether it is good or bad, they created it.

John F. Kennedy had this belief system. **Dan Rather** once said **Kennedy** became a true leader during the Bay of Pigs incident when he stood before the American people and said that Bay of Pigs was an atrocity that should never have happened, and then he took full responsibility for it.

When you really take responsibility, you are in power (always remember you have the capacity to choose life, choose love, choose health, choose happiness and sadness). On the contrary, when you avoid it, you get disempowered.

5.8 Ask questions that create pain and pleasure:

Leverage Exercise:

What is it costing me if I do not make a change now?

_____
_____
_____
_____
_____

What will it cost me in the future if I do not make this change now?

_____
_____
_____
_____
_____

What will be the immediate and long-term benefits if I make this change now?

_____
_____
_____
_____
_____

What kind of leverage can I create to ensure I will make this change?

_____
_____
_____
_____
_____

Notes:

PRINCIPLE 3

Changing Limiting Patterns
(changing focus, meaning, language, perception and physiology)

"You don't know who you are; you just know what they've told you about who you are!"
- MADDY MALHOTRA

6.1 Introduction:

All change is nothing but the interruption of patterns over and over again. To change someone's pattern, all you have to do is scramble the pattern. This is known as a **pattern interrupt**. The outcome is to consistently, appropriately and outrageously interrupt limiting, perceptual or behavioral patterns in order to create new choice for oneself and others at any moment in time.

We all have a place where we are extremely resourceful, so all change is really about taking resources from one area of your life and bringing them to an area where there are not enough resources. In this way, you will be able to handle anything.

By interrupting someone's patterns, you bring their resources to where they are needed. Then, once you get three, you can reinforce the new pattern. You have to condition the change so that it becomes automatic.

Breaking patterns is one of the most important skills to help create change. All the other change agent tools give you precise ways to sculpt a person after the old pattern is broken. However, you must have rapport, respect and connection to do so.

6.2 Three Primary Patterns to Break:

1) Patterns of Physiology

2) Patterns of Focus

3) Patterns of Language

The quickest way to change someone's state is to interrupt a **pattern of physiology**, for example:

- ➤ Temperature
- ➤ Body movement

- Facial expressions
- Pressure
- Proximity
- Speed of movement
- Tonality (voice)
- Tempo (voice)

The best way to interrupt someone's **pattern of focus** is to do or say something outside of what is generally acceptable in polite company. You can count on anything that is:

- Gross
- Humorous
- Confusing
- An overload to the system
- Weird expressions and sound

Remember – all pattern interrupts must be done under the umbrella of rapport. If you break rapport, you must gain it back immediately.

6.3 A few additional distinctions to remember when breaking patterns:
Questions are tools that help you understand what is going on and are a great resource for breaking patterns. The more outrageous and unexpected the question, the more effective it is .

Be aware:
Most of the things that control people are patterns that are primarily unconscious. Just by bringing them into a person's awareness, you become empowered to make a change. And when someone is aware, you can change things sooner.

Find the source:
Look for consistent emotional patterns that degrade the quality of a person's life. If you only change their behaviour without changing the emptional root,

the problem will simply relocate.

The source of a problem is always an emotional pattern of:

- Physiology
- Focus
- Language

Change the emotion by immediately breaking the pattern in each of these areas as soon as you become aware of what the person is doing. This gives them control over their emotional pattern and enables them to create a new set of empowering emotional habits.

Exercise:

Think of a negative emotional state you get into when you are upset, and brainstorm a few pattern interrupts you could use on yourself to break this state. Now, get yourself into that negative state and break your pattern. Have fun with it, and explore and practice a variety of ways to break your pattern.

_____
_____
_____
_____
_____
_____
_____
_____
_____
_____
_____
_____

Notes:

PRINCIPLE 4

Identify and define the problem (in solvable terms)

"If I had an hour to solve a problem, I'd spend 55 minutes thinking about the problem and five minutes thinking about solutions."
- ALBERT EINSTEIN

7.1 Introduction:

After you have begun to understand and appreciate a person's world, gotten some leverage, and interrupted a limiting pattern, you have now got to break a problem or challenge down to something that can be solved and achieved so that a person can find a new and better way to meet the needs he values the most.

People often trap themselves by making their problem much bigger than it is, or by defining their challenge in unresolvable terms. They are either so vague that they are unable to target the challenge, or they use language and beliefs that trigger certainty that change in impossible.

There are many different ways of defining and understanding what a person wants or needs to change, and the fastest way is to help them stop focusing on the problem and instead foucus on the outcome. As a leader, you can create massive change in people by helping them define their problems in resolvable terms. The key is to define the problem in a way that can be solved.

7.2 Keys to define the problem in solvable terms:

1) Define the problem. What do they really want?
2) Help a person define what is lost. What needs, or feelings need to be restored?
3) Look for what is really stopping them, not what they think is stopping them. This is where you will discover what they think is stopping them. This will help you discover what to redefine.

Often, the solutions can be found in changing the filter through which they are looking at it.

7.3 Pattern recongnition is power:

Before we begin to focus on a problem in definable or solvable terms, we must first understand how people's focus, thoughts, feelings, and ultimately actions contributed to the instigation of that problem to begin with. When working with people, the ability to recognize patterns allows you to get to the underlying source of the problem - the pattern - that often results in their success or failure, fulfilment or emptiness, happiness or disappointment in their lives. When you recognize a pattern, you can predict things, which enable you to anticipate and this anticipation is the competitive edge in life.

7.4 Identifying patterns:

We all have the same six needs, but what makes people different is how they go about getting them and, as we have discussed, how they go about getting their needs is based upon a model of the world, a set of beliefs, a set of principles, a set of values, and a set of rules.

When you have significant events that affect your nervous system, your brain begins to try and figure out where that effect came from and it develops a plan to either duplicate that effect if it is pleasurable, or avoid it if it causes pain. People's model of the world, their way of thinking and believing, and additional references they have contribute to the decisions they make about how to feel, act or react, and thus from their model of the world and their life experiences, patterns are shaped, often without awareness of what those patterns are or the effect they have on their lives. The first step to pattern-recognition is to identify patterns that we may be running and whether they are positive, netural or negative.

7.5 Pattern utilization and creation:

Once you understand the pattern a person is running, you can then utilize that pattern to create a change. Perhaps you can help people notice a pattern that creates tremendous success in their lives.

Can they utilize that pattern in other areas? Or maybe they have a destructive pattern, you can help them break that pattern and then replace it with a more empowering one.

The more you become aware of and practice identifying patterns, the more likely you will be able to actually create new patterns. You can create patterns by exploring what has worked for others, what has worked for you in the past or by anticipating what will work in the future.

7.6 Natural steps to pattern creation:

1) **Recognize** the patterns

2) **Apply** patterns

3) **Create** your own patterns

If you are going to be a leader, you must be able to affect people at many different levels. To do so, you have to develop your own personal mastery.

7.7 Level of personal mastery:

1) Change your state in a moment.
Lead yourself, take yourself from a state where you are overwhelmed, tired, frustrated, burnt-out, angry, sad and change it in a hearbeat.

2) Change your state in an environment or a context.
Make your worst your best. Be able to change yourself in a difficult situation by linking it to a situation that puts you in a great state. Take another individual and help them change.

3) Live in a peak state.
Create a peak state or model of the world. Spend the majority of your time feeling centered, strong and fulfilled. When you are able to do all three of these things with group of people simultaneously, you will have achieved a level of not only personal mastery, but also masterful leadership.

7.8 Sample questions that access new resources:

The following questions are designed to cause you to experience more happiness, excitement, pride, gratitude, joy, commitment and love in everyday of your life. Remember, quality questions create a quality life.

Become fully associated and come up with two or three answers to all of these questions. If you have difficulty discovering an answer, simply add the word could.

Example: "What could I be most happy about in my life now?"

Problem-solving questions:
1) What can I learn from this?
2) What is great about this?
3) What is not perfect yet?
4) What am I willing to do to make it the way I want it?
5) What am I willing to not to make it the way I want it?
6) How can I enjoy the process?

Morning power questions:
1) What am I happy about in my life right now?
2) What am I excited about in my life right now?
3) What am I proud of in my life right now?
4) What am I grateful for in my life right now?
5) What am I enjoying in my life right now?
6) What am I committed to in my life right now?
7) Who do I love? Who loves me?

Evening questions:
1) What have you given today?
2) What did I learn today?
3) How has today added to the quality of my life?

Notes:

PRINCIPLE 5

Make the Change and Find Empowering Alternative Resources.

(Access empowering ways to meet your six human needs and the emotions you need to strengthen)

"The journey of a thousand miles begins with one step."
- LAO TZU

8.1 Introduction:

If you are going to change a behaviour, thought process or action, first you have to interrupt the old pattern and then you have to give the person something new that meets the same needs. In other words, you cannot just stop doing something; you have to start doing something else in that place.

Creating new alternative empowers a person to find all the options that are available, thus creating multiple ways to meet their needs. There are unlimited alternatives found within a person's imagination, creativity and history that can be used to create new physiologies, focus, questions, language, beliefs and meanings.

One simple, yet powerful, empowering alternative is transforming the language we use, using transformational vocabulary.

8.2 The power of words:

When two people meet, words actually have the least amount of impact on how a person feels about the other. According to research done by Albert Mehrabian, Professor Emeritus in psychology at UCLA, words comprise only 7% of communication. In fact, 55% of communication is visual (body language, eye contract) and 38% is vocal (pitch, speed, volume, tone of voice).

Physiology and tonality are far more important in this regard. However, words have an unbelievable power in how they affect your own set of beliefs.

In fact, the words you use from moment to moment shape your destiny. Words can make you laugh and cry, wound and heal. They can change the way you think and feel in an instant. Just one word can change your state by creating a biochemical effect on your body.

8.3 Words create Beliefs:

The words that you use consistently shape who you are. Your brain is constantly creating shortcuts to make decision more quickly. These shortcuts become your belief system, comprised of a series of generalizations of your life experience so far. However, the generalizations that you create can either empower or disempower you.

As belief is made up of words, when you change one word, you can actually change the whole meaning.

According to Compton's Encyclopedia, the English language contains some 5,00,000 words. Yet, the average person's working vocabulary consists of only 2,000 – 0.5% of the entire language. So, how many words make up our habitual vocabulary?

For most people, it averages around 200–300 words. (By contrast, John Milton's writings used about 17,000 words and William Shakespeare used 24,000 words, 5,000 of which he only used one time.) Of those 5,00,000 words, about 3,000 are used to describe emotions, two-thirds of which are used to describe negative emotions.

With all of these readily-available ways to express our feelings and ideas, why are we comfortable with such an impoverished vocabulary? We generally use the same vocabulary over and over again. In the pursuit of efficiency, we often create shortcuts that can short-change us emotionally.

8.4 Listen to your word-choices:

Use this technology as a diagnostic tool when you are working with other people. Look at their physiology and listen for words that are creating limits as they speak or think out loud.

8.5 Exercise:

How do these words feel different?

Angry	Peeved
Chivalry	Good manners
Passion	Feels good

Defusing negative words/phrases:

Angry	To	Unhappy
Depressed	To	Calm before action
Failed	To	Learning
I hate	To	Prefer
Irriated	To	Stimulated
Overwhelmed	To	Popular
Rejected	To	Misunderstood
Lonely	To	Unoccupied

Increasing positive words/phrases:

Comfortable	To	Smashing
Determined	To	Unstoppable
Failed	To	Learning

I hate	To	I prefer
Rejected	To	Misunderstand
Lonely	To	Unoccupied

Amplifying positive words/phrases:

Comfortable		Smashing
Determined		Unstoppable
Fast		Ballistic
Fortunate		Unbelievable
Great		Phenomenal
Interested		Relish
Smart		Brilliant
Good		Ecstatic

Summary:

These words are the building blocks of human experience. And, the words that you use habitually are shaping you – your beliefs, the way you think and what you do.

Expand your vocabulary; expand your life.

Notes:

PRINCIPLE 6

Condition the change until it becomes a habit.

(Condition new decisions, thoughts, emotions and actions)

"Character isn't something you were born with and can't change, like your fingerprints. It's something you weren't born with and must take responsibility for forming."
- JIM ROHN

9.1 Introduction:

When creating change, you must know that any positive change will last beyond the moment and will stick in the future. A pattern will not stick just because you had a conversation; you have to condition the pattern and create reinforcement. Any thought, feeling, emotion, behaviour or belief that is consistently reinforced will become conditioned.

Designer anchors are the opposite of unconscious anchors – they are ones we make ourselves to empower us. Once we have created them, we can use them to produce the state of mind or mood we need. For instance, you enter an interview calm and relaxed because you have triggered the appropriate anchor.

9.2 To create an anchor:

Whether or not we are consciously aware of it, we are constantly creating anchors to certain situations, people and experiences. When you are in an intense state, it will get linked to anything unique that is consistently happening at that time.

Type of anchors:

- Touch
- Sound
- Smell
- Visual

Step 1 - Either catch the person in a peak state or put the person in a peak state.

Step 2 - At the peak state, consistently do something unique.

Test to see if it works by:

Step 3 - Interrupting their pattern.

Step 4 – Re-firing the trigger.

9.3 Keys for an anchor to work:

Key 1 - Make sure there is an intense emotional state.
This is the most important factor. If a person is laughing hysterically, you can fire the anchor 10 years from now and it will still work. However, if a person is barely laughing and you anchor them, that anchor might not even last a minute.

Key 2 - Create it at the peak of the experience.
For an anchor to work, it must be done at the peak of an experience. Trust your instincts to find the right moment. Your unconscious mind has more power than your conscious mind – trust it !

Key 3 - Create a unique trigger.
Make sure the type of anchor you choose is different enough to break the pattern, but not so strange that it may trigger an inappropriate reaction for the person in a certain situation.

Key 4 - Be able to effectively relicate the anchor.
It will not fire off again later unless you replicate it identically.

9.4 - Some Tips:
The anchors (or anchor) should be fired in exactly the same way every time you link them to the resourceful experience. For an instance, touch the little finger knuckle of the left hand in exactly the same way each time.

An anchor, as a resource state, is growing and stoping at its highest point. If you do not experience the state when future pacing and especially if you experience anxiety, then stop applying the anchor. (You don't want to anchor the negative state!). Repeat the steps above to establish the anchor.

There is a knowingness which makes anchoring work that is established by the unconscious mind.

You can strengthen the anchor by repeating the above process over several days.

If you are in a situation where you experience the desired state in reality, then you can re-establish the anchor to that situation.

9.5 Another tool to condition any change is incantation.

Incantations are when you say something out loud with absolute certainty and you repeat it again and again until you begin to believe it.

Remember, incantations are expressed with emotional energy, intensity and conviction, which is also known as being in a "Peak State." It's best to do your incantations while standing, or even better while jogging or working out; and say them out loud. Doing so will help ensure that the meanings and the intentions of the words you are uttering become locked into the nervous system and sink deeply into the subconscious mind, bringing about lasting and powerful life-changes.

Incantations:

Now I am the voice.

I am leading not following.

I am belief, not doubt.

I am creating, not destroying.

I am a force for good.

I am a force for god.

I am a leader

"All I need is within me now and I have the courage to see it through."

"I love my life and I am so blessed."

"When you open your eyes in the morning, say to yourself, "I choose happiness today. I choose success today. I choose the right actions today. I choose love and goodwill for all today. I choose peace today." Pour life, love, and interest into this affirmation and you have chosen happiness."

– Joseph Murphy

"You are as young as you think you are. You are as strong as you think you are. You are as useful as you think you are. You are as young as your thoughts."

– Joseph Murphy

"Your subconscious mind is the builder of your body and is on the job 24 hours a day. You interfere with its life-giving patterns by negative thinking."

– Joseph Murphy

"Suppose you are afraid of water, a mountain, an interview, an audition, or you fear closed spaces. If you are afraid of swimming, begin now to sit still for five or ten minutes three or four times a day, and imagine you are swimming. Actually, you are swimming in your mind. It is a subjective experience. Mentally, you have projected yourself into the water. You feel the chill of water and the movement of your arms and legs. It is all real, vivid, and a joyous activity of the mind. It is not idle day-dreaming, for you know that what you are experiencing in your imagination will be developed in your subconscious mind. Then, you will be compelled to express the image and likeness of the picture you impressed on your deeper mind. This is the law of the subconscious. You could apply the same technique if you are afraid of mountains, or high places. Imagine you are climbing the mountain, feel the reality of it all, enjoy the scenery, knowing that as you continue to do this mentally, you will do it physically with ease and comfort."

– Joseph Murphy

"Never use the terms - I can't afford it or I can't do this. Your subconscious mind takes you at your word and sees to it that you do not have the money or the ability to do what you want to do. Affirm - I can do all the things through the power of my subconscious mind."

– Joseph Murphy

Notes:

PRINCIPLE 7

Associate with higher purpose and connect to an Empowering Environment
(Make sure the environment supports it)

"Life is most persistent and urgent question is, what are you doing for others."
- MARTIN LUTHER KING JR.

10.1 Introduction:

When creating change, you must relate this change to a person's highest values and help them integrate their new empowering alternatives into the environment where they actually live and thrive. The goal is to make sure the person is strong enough that even if the environment is extremely harsh, the change will last. You also want to make sure they can create an environment that supports their change and helps them understand how the change relates to what they value the most and what they ultimately want to accomplish.

10.2 The importance of standards and peer group:

The standards that people have for themselves and the standards of their peer group, massively affect whether the change they have made will last. For change to last, it is vital for people to surround themselves with a peer group that will hold them to higher standards, as well as create those standards within themselves.

10.3 The quality of your life is a direct reflection of the expectations of your peer group:

How can we help others create an empowering peer group?

We can encourage them to;

Create an environment that supports them (like throwing away all the junk food in the house).

Join an organization or group.

Get an accountability partner (like a physical trainer or gym buddy).

Help them identify a role model or mentor they can connect with.

10.4 The power of identity:

The strongest force in the human soul is the need to remain consistent with our own definition of ourselves - our identity. In other words, once we decide who we are as a person, then we will give ourselves no choice but to find a way to be consistent with that perception. However, many of us settle for an identity that is less than our true capability, so our job as leaders is to help others raise and expand their identity.

10.5 Prriya Kaur's 7 principles for transforming identity:

1) Give a person an experience that transforms his identity:

For example, if a person believes he is boring, give him an experience of something exciting and then anchor the feelings and beliefs that being exciting or adventurous is indeed a part of his identity.

2) Create a change in physiology:

As we mentioned before, physiology is the filter through which we interpret all information, including beliefs we have about who we are. For example, if you train a person how to use his body in a more empowering way (like standing with his shoulders back, head high and so on), then he will feel and experience life in a completely different way.

3) Get them to live in an emotional state that empowers them:

For example, get them to live in passionate states, courageous states, playful states or loving states. Remember, pain only motivates a person to make a change in the moment, but pleasure is a long-term motivator. If you can get others to access states that consistently make them feel good, no matter what the environment is, they will want to continue living this way.

4) Enhance and affirm their identity through incantations:

What is great about using an incantation to affirm identity is that it uses all of the Triad. It utilizes physiology, focus, language and meaning.

5) Use positive reinforcement:

Catch them doing things right and celebrate, which also shapes their identity through anchoring.

6) Provide for them a more compelling future:

When people believe they have a future, that alone shifts the perception of who they are.

7) Help them master another skill:

As people feel they have mastered a skill, it gives them a sense of growth, and as they grow, their identity expands.

So, you have many ways to help a person build an identity and you can also use these to expand your own identity as a leader. You can greatly influence change by being a leader, the one who sets the standard in a peer's group. When you have a standard that's higher than anybody else in the group, that's what really makes you a leader.

Notes:

MEASURING YOURSELF AS A LEADER

(Use feedback that you get from yourself and from other people to greater depth of scale for impacting people)

"Leaders become great, not because of their power, but because of their ability to empower others."
- JOHN C. MAXWELL

11.1 Introduction:

Level 1. At the moment, can change from undesired to the desired state, create a shift (Triad shift), emotional change, behaviour change, action in a moment change.

Level 2. Create influence that creates lasting change in a challenging context through time, requires conditioning of a new Triad.

Level 3. Creating an influence that shifts the person's whole life across multiple contexts and time periods. Expand their model of the world, it's driving force, guiding force, fuel of choice.

Leve 4. You influence someone to influence others for the greater good (Jesus, Gandhi, Muhammad and so on).

You can only influence someone to the level of depth you have mastered.

11.2 Where are you on the scale of your leadership mastery?

How deep is your level of leadership?

Level 1 (moment)	1X1 ?
Level 2 (changing context)	1X2 ?
Level 3 (across context)	2X2 ?
Level 4 (others for greater good)	1X3 ?

Where are you on the scale of influence ?

Level 1 (moment)	1X1 ? you are able to influence yourself consistently for the greater good
Level 2 (changing context)	1X2 ? you can lead
Level 3 (across context)	2X2 ? you have the ability to consistently and simultaneously influence a large number of people
Level 4 (others for greater good)	1X3 ? you create a culture

Level 1: Leadership in the moment. You have the ability to change any person in a moment from undesired state to a desired state.

Level 2: Change the context you can make the change from an undesired state not just in the moment but also through time in the context.

Level 3: Change the level of life. You can change their model of the world and set a standard that creates an identity so people treat them differently in multiple context throughout time.

Level 4: Shift others' level of respect for humanity. You have the ability to influence someone that they shift their model of the world so that they can do it for someone else.

11.4 Exercise:

What are you on the scale of leadership expertise if you are really honest with yourself?

_____

_____

_____

What is your level of expertise in terms of scale?

Where is your current level of gravity? Where do you live consistently?

11.5 Secrets of leadership Expertise:

Be totally honest with yourself; know where you really are in your ability to lead.

It does not matter where you start; what matters is knowing where you are because if you know where you are and you decide the level of leadership you want to go, you can change.

Go deep! Most people try to go wide before they have gone deep. Do not make this mistake.

CONGRATULATIONS

Wow! You have completed the Leadership Expertise course successfully. I am sure it will help generate leadership skills within you and help master the already existing skills.

References:

Jago, A.G. (1982). Leadership: Perspectives in theory and research. Journal of Management Science 28(3) 315-332.

Northouse, P. G. (2007). Leadership theory and practice (4th ed.). Thousand Oaks, CA, US: Sage Publications, Inc

Hersey, P., & Blanchard, K. H. (1988). Management and Organizational Behavior. Englewood Cliffs, NJ: Prentice-Hall.

Zaccaro, S. J., Kemp, C., & Bader, P. (2004). Leader traits and attributes. In J. Antonakis, A. T. Cianciolo, & R. J. Sternberg (Eds.). The nature of leadership (pp. 101-124). Thousand Oaks, CA: Sage.

Antonakis, J,. Cianciolo, A., and Sternberg, R. J. (2004). The nature of leadership. Thousand Oaks, CA: Sage Publications.

Bennis, W. (1994). On becoming a leader. (Rev. ed). Reading, MA: Perseus Books.

Chance, P. L, Chance, E. W. (2002). Introduction to educational leadership & organizational behavior: theory into practice. NY.

DuBrin, A. J. (2009). Leadership: Research findings, practice, and skills. Boston: Houghton Mifflin.

Gardner, H. (1975). The shattered mind. New York: Knopf.

Goldberg, L. R. (1993). The structure of phenotypic personality traits. American Psychologist, 48, 26-34.

Goleman, D. (1995). Emotional intelligence. New York: Bantam.

Hein, S. Emotional Intelligence. http://eqi.org/

Judge, T. A., Bono, J. E., Ilies, R. and Gerhardt, M. W. 82002). Personality and leadership: A qualitative and quantitative review. Journal of Applied Psychology, 87, 765-780.

Kirkpatrick, S. & Locke, E. (1991). Leadership: Do traits matter? Academy of Management Executive, May, 48-60.

Knes, M. (2009). Leadership. In Encyclopedia of Business.

http://www.enotes.com/biz-encyclopedia/leadership

Lord, R.G., De Vader, C.L., & Alliger, G.M. (1986). A meta-analysis of the relation between personality traits and leadership perceptions: An application of validity generalization procedures. Journal of Applied Psychology, 71(3), 402-410.

Mann, R. D. (1959). A review of the relationship between personality and performance in small groups. Psychological Bulletin, 66 (4), 241-70.

McCaffery, P. (2004). The higher education manager's handbook: Effective leadership and management in universities and colleges. London: Routledge Farmer.

Merriam-Webster Online Dictionary
http://www.merriam-webster.com/dictionary/sociability

Northouse, P. G. (2007). Leadership: theory and practice. 4th ed. Thousand Oaks, CA: Sage Publications.

Salovey, P., & Mayer, J. (1990). Emotional intelligence. Imagination, cognition, and personality, 9(3), 185-211.

Stanford Encyclopedia of Philosophy http://plato.stanford.edu/entries/integrity/

Stogdill, R. (1974). Handbook of leadership - A survey of theory and research. New York.

Stogdill, R. M. (1948). Personal factors associated with leadership: A survey of the literature. Journal of Psychology, 25, 35-71.

Zaccaro, S. J., Kemp, C., & Bader, P. (2004). Leader traits and attributes. In J. Antonakis, A. T. Cianciolo, & R. J. Sternberg (Eds.). The nature of leadership (pp. 101-124). Thousand Oaks, CA: Sage.

Porter, D. (2012). How to Use the Power of Leverage to Achieve More. Dr Jim Porter.

www.ingramcontent.com/pod-product-compliance
Lightning Source LLC
Chambersburg PA
CBHW060434220526

45465CB00008B/3133